Living IN A Dying Land

Living IN A Dying Land

WILLIAM EPPS JR.

Printed in the United States of America
ISBN 978-1-958434-78-9 (sc)
ISBN 978-1-958434-79-6 (e)

2023.02.02

MainSpring Books
5901 W. Century Blvd
Suite 750
Los Angeles, CA, US, 90045

www.mainspringbooks.com

We have taken on the sin of Adam who disobeyed the word of God. When we do not listen to what God has to say, we always fall short of his blessings.

Adam had everything that he needed in the garden to supply his every need. God came into the garden in the cool of the day and talked to Adam to make sure that all is well with him.

There was one river that ran out of Eden, eastward to the garden to water it. The river is split in four parts: the first part is Pison which encompasses the whole land of Havilah where there's gold; the second river is Gihon, which encompasses the whole land of Ethiopia, where Ham's son Cush lives; the third river is Hiddekel, which goes east of Assyria; and the fourth is the Euphrates river where the four angels are stationed—Syria, Iran, Iraq, and Turkey.

The garden of Eden was a very large place. Adam had full range of all this ground. I looked at all this ground that Adam had to cover. He did not have a car, boat, nor airplane to cover this ground.

God spoke everything into being, but he created Adam in his own likeness. How special is man that God has made him? Throughout time, God always had something special for man. Because He loved man, He promised man a savior. We need to thank God for the past, present, and the future. Luke 21 says:

Jesus gave his disciples a glimpse of what it would be like at the end of time. Just look back at the Apostle Paul's description of the time of the end. When we read the scriptures and then look back at what's going on in the world today, it really makes us wonder if we are living in the end time.

Satan is on his game working to derail what God has set into motion. Jesus promised us that he would return to Earth to reward the righteous and to judge the unrighteous. First Samuel is divided into three parts: 1-7, dealing with Samuel; 8-15, dealing with Saul, 16-31, dealing with David.

First Kings was written by Solomon 400 years before the seven wise men of Greece wrote it. First Chronicle is the history of the Jewish nation written by Ezra; the book of Job was written by Moses, a poetry book; Job 3 says let this day perish from which I was born.

Jesus wanted us to know what was said about him in the Old Testament will come to pass in the New Testament. At the time when the Old Testament was written, 40 Authors had instructions from God to write the Word of God. There was no confusion at the place where they were writing, they all were on one accord.

In the land of the dying, we will stay here until our race is finished. I often wonder why there's so much confusion in the churches today. We argue about who is right in the house of prayer. The Preacher is the Bible, the members are the hymn book and the articles of faith.

God's master plan did not need any alterations because God did not need no one to remind him. He wanted man to be on the same page as well. God wanted man to know that he will be there with him to the end. What a great thing to know that God is with you. We can't get around this trap called sin because it was passed down to us. I am glad that this is only a temporary thing for a reason because we are sojourners down here. Jesus went out on Calvary hill one Friday from the sixth to the ninth hour and covered it all, from noon until 3pm. We are just traveling through this land of the dying, on our way to that place where we will never die again. We walk through the valley of the shadow of death. We fear no evil because God is with us, his rod and staff comfort us. God told us to put our trust in him.

Satan wants us to believe that God's Word was not aimed directly at us. He wanted to keep us hoodwinked and blind about the true Word of God.

We see how he threw a slider to Eve, and she fell for it, and passed it on to Adam. Now that's where the rubber met the road. We can't fool God at all because He made us and He know our thoughts before we can babble them out. The devil can't get to the heart, but he sure can rattle the head, that's what he did to

Job. He made him curse the day that he was born. The devil wanted man to die a physical and a spiritual death.

Physical death means we will be away from God. Spiritual is where we would spend eternity. We need to choose what's the right one that we can be sure of.

I came up with an idea of missing heaven by 16 inches. The distance from the brain to the heart is 16 inches. If we do not think about it or receive it, we will miss heaven by 16 inches.

We need to listen to what God is saying then we can walk in the newness of life with no problems. If we know how to comprehend what God is saying to us, then God will give us clear understandings of the what, the when, the where, the how, and the why. We are only limited to five senses that's why we can't elevate above this level. Until we get up above this place called Earth, then our mind will be open, and we will know it all.

Some of us think that we are going to heaven and that we are no longer of any use on earth. But heaven is a place that God has promised us as a reward for traveling through this land of sin. God will not go back on his word. God's word stands all by itself that we can count on.

We can count on God for our every need. Just trust Him. He will not let you down, nor will He forget. You do not have to make an appointment. His ear is always open for you. He sent His Son Jesus to bail us from sin. Satan has a real choke hold on us. We could not see the forest for the trees, thank God for Jesus who made the way for us to see things clear again.

God has given us the characteristics of the heavens. The first heaven is the atmosphere of the birds where we get our oxygen. Second, heaven consists of the sun, moon and the stars. The third heaven is where God resides. Jesus has two things in mind for man: He is praying for man, and He is building a new home called New Jerusalem where he and man would live forever.

A question was brought up. How do you know that He who He said that He is? My answer to them is read the Word and it will open your knowledge and understanding. I tell them to read John 14 because God said, "If it were not so, I would have told you." So, read and understand. Each morning, we rise, and God gives us a glimpse of his holy power when we look out on the dawn of a new day. We can't make sunshine, nor can we make rain. We can't make the wind blow. Satan is always trying to pull the carpet out from under you and pull you down for the count. A good Christian never runs from the fight. He always squares up his shoulders and take the hits.

We need to be sure that each piece of the armor is fitting and ready for battle. Each piece was made at the cross by the finished works of Jesus.

I was in search of happiness. God granted me peace of mind. He opened my knowledge and understanding to stay focus on him. He put a lamp upon my feet and a light upon my pathway. He put joy in my heart and opened my eyes so that I can see things that is set before me. I know Satan has some wind in his jaws with me for writing these things, but I am living for God. We all need to speak up for God and put Satan in that dark whole that's made for him.

Let us look at how God made Abraham the progenitor of three black nations: the Israelites, the Ishmaelites, and the Midianites (Genesis 17:58). God gave Moses three codes in Exodus: the first code (Exodus 21:22) is a moral code dealing with judgment and the law; the second code (Exodus 23) is a spiritual code dealing with Christ and salvation; and the third code (Exodus 24:10) is a special code that God gave to Moses and the elders because they saw the everlasting sign of God.

God always give His people a sign to look for His coming. We can only see so far. Now look up and see the sky. Isn't that amazing. God gave man the key to happiness by saying love ye one another as I have love you. Love is the key that makes a person forgive his brother and ask for forgiveness.

God is very angry with man on how he is carrying on with what God has entrusted him with. I will say that it's like casting the pearls into the pig pen, you know that can be a royal mess. God said in the days of Noah that he had grieved over the fact that he had made man and beast and was going to wipe them off the face of the earth. However, Noah pleaded with the Lord, asking him to give mankind another chance. 120 years later, all evil men were done away with, but sin still reared its ugly head.

God does not like sin, and he sees the blood of Jesus that covered our sins at Calvary. He hates sin, but he still loves the sinner because the sinner can repent.

God always had a plan for man to follow, but Satan came with a detour sign to make things more complex. From Genesis to Revelation, Satan has tried to block God's plan, but no matter how hard Satan tries to stop it, he will always fail because God is all-powerful.

From Adam to Malachi, there was not one person who could say "Lord, send me, I will go for you."

The Old Testament was written by 40 authors over a period of 1600 years. These authors were kings, princes, poets, and philosophers.

From Adam to Abraham, the history of the human race is recorded. Zechariah was born in Babylon, and his name means "Jehovah remembers." Zechariah received ten visions on the same night.

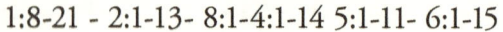
1:8-21 - 2:1-13- 8:1-4:1-14 5:1-11- 6:1-15

Let's look at how God spoke to Moses. He told them to camp between Migdol and the sea. Hagar was forced into the desert with her son to die of thirst. We see how Joseph wanted to fulfill his divine dream. he was sold as a slave and put in prison down in Egypt.

We see how Moses was caught between the Egyptian royalty and the affliction with God's people. We see how David was anointed by Samuel, how Hezekiah was seeking a revival and was trapped by a powerful army. The disciples sailed to Galilee, and now we look at how the Red Sea was opened so the children of Israel could walk over on dry ground. We often want Jesus to give us what we want right now, but the time will come when Jesus takes the tares away from the wheat. This will happen when the fullness of time has come. Christians are not judged on Earth because they are carrying the Gospel of Jesus Christ, they will be rewarded for their great deeds.

Satan wants to be the ruler of mankind. If he stands toe to toe to God, what more do you think that he would do to us. In the Old Testament, we see that God was down on man because of man's sinful nature. God shut heaven for 400 years. No communication at all from God to man nor did man try to reach God.

Sin was off the chain. God waited until the fullness of time to take care of this matter. God had and will have the last say so of this situation.

A question was raised: Why did God make the devil? The devil was made to keep man in check. The devil will make you focus on God because the devil knows how to put an old fashion whipping on you.

We walk by faith because faith is the substance of things hoped for and the evidence of things not seen. We give all our worries and problems to God, and he will fix them for us. Just think about what God had in store for Adam if he hadn't taken his eyes off God and listened to another voice. God had promised Adam that he was in full control. Satan was jealous because Adam was receiving so much attention from God. This caused Satan to become unbalanced and lose control. God was very happy with his masterpiece because man was made in the very likeness of God.

Adam was given open mind and he was given the ability to name everything on Earth. Now how about that for a brain. I can say that God wrote Adam a blank check in the garden for everything except the tree of good and evil. We look throughout the Bible, and we see where many men have sinned because of what Adam left on the drawing board.

The Old Testament records the sinful things that man has found himself in. Adam, the first man, was the first to sin, and his son, Cain, was the second because he killed his brother, Abel. Let us look at how the Old Testament started off. In the beginning, God created the world and all that is in it. We see how Genesis closes with the story of Joseph, living in a coffin in Egypt, the land of the dying.

Now, let us look at how the Old Testament ended. It ends with a curse on the land, as well as on the people who had turned away from God.

We see how Satan can twist and misunderstand the true meaning of God's word. He uses just one word to mislead and deceive.

We look at this low, sorrowful land as a dressing room where we prepare to leave for our eternal home, the New Jerusalem. We will not leave here until our work is finished down here in the land of the dying. Jesus told us that He will never leave us. Now that's a bright light in a dark room. Biblical history takes us to the unknown future.

The book of Revelation is filled with symbols and future events. The word apocalypse means to take away or to unveil. Revelation is all about Jesus being the author of this book. We see clearly that Jesus gave this information to the angels, and how the angels communicated it to John. John then wrote it in a book and sent it to the seven churches in Asia. Jesus told John to write the things that he has seen, things of the past, the things which are, the present, and things that come after, future things.

We see that Revelation reveals the human side of Jesus and the Deity of Jesus being God on the Throne. It shows the Eternal side of Jesus being Alpha and Omega, the first and the last, the who was, the who is, and the who is to come.

We see how John had many references of the Old Testament. John looked at Exodus, Isaiah, Jeremiah, Ezekiel, Daniel, and Zechariah. John gives a threefold focus on Jesus in Revelation 1:5-6, highlighting Christ as the faithful witness, the firstborn of the dead, and the ruler of the kings of the Earth. The four living creatures sing the hymn of Creation to God, because He is the Lord God Almighty. They worship God for his Holiness and his Omnipotence because he is all Powerful, they also worship God for his Eternality.

The seven horns and the seven eyes are the seven Spirits of God in all the earth. The seven horns refer to Jesus' Omnipotence. The horns represent power. Seven is the Biblical number of completions. The seven eyes are Jesus' Omniscience and Divine Wisdom while the seven Spirits of God represent the Holy Spirit and his Divine attributes. The tribulation and its purpose: the first purpose are the salvation of the elect, and the second purpose is the condemnation of the lost. The seven seals are the judgments. The seven trumpets are more devastating than the seven seals The seven bowls judgment is called the plagues, because they are the last. Then the wrath of God is finished.

We see the battle of Armageddon and the second coming of Christ. Russia is said to lead the battle of Armageddon, as described in Ezekiel 38:1-7.

The seven bowl judgments are poured out on those who have the mark of the beast and those who worship his image. The people who are saved at the time of the tribulation will not have to worry about God's wrath.

We see that Revelation is not written in chronological order. Some of Revelation is dealing with Daniel, and some is dealing with Joseph. John told of his first vision in which he saw the Lamb of God, who is Jesus, standing on Mount Zion. He had the 144,000 with him and they were singing a new song that no one knew except for the 144,000. The name of Mount Zion was changed to Jerusalem.

John then focused on Mark 4 and saw Jesus standing there with the 144,000. He heard and saw an angel flying around in heaven, preaching the gospel to those on Earth. The gospel is eternal. People of all nations and languages, let's look at the first book of the Bible and how it shows us how God created the heaven where His throne is. He oversees the whole universe from this heaven, and there are many angels there. God created love and joy after he created these angels. He gave them free choice.

The highest angel was called Lucifer, the one who shines as bright as the morning. He was the one that stood in the presence of God. God told Lucifer in Ezekiel 28:14 that he had ordained him and put on the Holy Mount. Now in verse 12, God told Lucifer that he is the perfection of wisdom and perfect in beauty. Lucifer got all puffed up in his beauty and wisdom he went down as fast as he was elevated.

There were two others that was equal to God in heaven: Jesus and the Holy Spirit. Ezekiel 28:17 says that Lucifer's heart and wisdom was corrupted. In Ezekiel 28:15, God told Satan that he was blameless until wickedness was found in him. Isaiah 14:12-14 reveals the things that Satan said he will do.

The Patriarchs and the Prophets—of all the holy, there stood one called Enoch, seven generations from Adam. Enoch walked with God and was not seen, because God took him. Genesis 5:24 says that Enoch was transformed and taken from the earth without seeing death. Just look at how Enoch was living in the land of the dying. Enoch was missed on Earth, but God had a more important lesson to teach his people still on Earth.

The instructions which God gave to Adam was repeated by Seth. Enoch's translation brought hope to the faithful still on Earth.

That the righteous will have a reward, just as the wicked will have final punishment. Enoch's life shows that it is possible to keep God's commands and resist temptation. Enoch's translation was to be enjoyed by God's faithful followers. Now, God's grace is twofold: it is forgiveness and pardon for who we are, and forgiveness for the sins we commit. God stepped in and had a worldwide flood, and Noah and his family carried the sin across to the other side of the flood, choosing to turn against God.

These followers of Satan scattered out over the earth and settled, building the great Tower of Babel. God has a special plan for Israel on how he would choose them to show the unbelieving nations of his love and grace. God went from Adam to Seth and up through the patriarchs Enoch, and on up the line to Jacob. The steps of a good man are ordered by the Lord. Its not how many times a man falls or how many times he gets back up. We have all types of problems—big, small and all in between. There will always be a storm in your life. You are getting ready to go into a storm you are already in a storm or you're just coming out of a storm.

Don't focus on what people say or think. Just keep your eyes focused on God. Sometimes we trip over our own feet for not paying attention.

Let's take a close look at evangelism—how and where it started. The angel Gabriel came unto the shepherds while they were in the field watching over their flocks. He then made this announcement: Unto you this day, in the city of David, a Savior is being born. The shepherds said let us go and see this that has come to pass. The shepherds were the first to evangelize of the good news.

They followed the star to Bethlehem where they saw the Savior of the world. We need to get the Word of God out into a dying world.

The wise men also saw the star over Bethlehem. They followed it to the place where Jesus lay.

Now we can fast track to the place where Jesus' ministry and His life coming to an end on that old cross from the 6th to the 9th hour, from 12 noon until 3pm. Jesus saw that everything was done, and he gave up the ghost. Simon the Cyrene carried the cross for Jesus, and this took him to the right side of truth and salvation. The thief on the right side of Jesus was also taken to his place, to the right.

Before Jesus left for heaven, He began a new and spiritual Israel, inviting everyone to follow Him. Jesus established His church and His followers who would carry the name of Christ. That's how the word Christians came to be by being a follower of Christ. Thousands were converted in one day. God's love was clearly seen at the cross, His giving of His self was not for the people who deserved it, but for those who really needed it. God loves them because He had made them in His likeness. He would give His life to save them. Satan's doom was sealed because Satan would lose the great controversy between Christ and himself. Satan is now wounded.

And the seals are recorded in Revelation 8:5. The second account, from Revelation 8:2 through 11:19, describes many events leading up to the second coming of Jesus. The third account in Revelation 12 offers a different perspective and reveals more events. Revelation 12:14 tells us the story of the event that will lead to the dramatic unveiling of Jesus. The fourth account, Revelation will start all over again. Revelation 15 records the seven vials and it concludes in Revelation 19. The second piece of information, the things you have seen, the things which are, the things that are, the things that will come after.

The seven candlesticks are the seven churches, the mystery of the Stars and the seven golden candlesticks. Revelation is a great symbolic book. It is written in symbols to be understood. The seven stars and the seven candlesticks are for us. The seven stars are the seven angels, the pastors, and the seven candlesticks are the seven churches. The oil flows through the candlesticks as the Spirit of God flows through the churches. In Revelation 2 and 3, we have seen things of the past and are looking at things of the present. We will follow John into the future to see what will come to pass in the future. John enters the prophetic portion of the book of Revelation.

Revelation 5:8-10 tells us that the 24 elders will be a part of the first resurrection. Daniel 7:21 reveals information about the Kingdom of God and who will reign with Jesus. The church is built on the foundation of the Apostles and the Prophets. The 12 Apostles in the New Testament and the 12 tribes of Israel in the Old Testament.

The Godhead and the mystery of it, the greatest mystery, Jesus being the root of David. John 1:1 says that in the beginning was the Word, the Word was with God, and the Word was God. He spoke all things into motion, and the Holly men wrote the Word of God as H directed to do so, the word Emmanuel means God with us. The Godhead is a mystery. It demonstrates when God became human, and the Scripture says that the Wisdom of God is a mystery, the Prophecy of the seven seals is one of the most incredible prophecies in the entire Bible.

The four horsemen of the apocalypse are often interpreted as representing the spread of war, famine, and death. Some people believe that the red horse represents communism, the black horse represents capitalism, the white horse represents Catholicism, and the pale horse represents Islam.

The theme of Revelation is "behold, he cometh with the clouds." We need to be sure that we will be in the right harvest of the wheat and be on guard, looking for Jesus's second coming. God's word is telling us to be ready.

God told John to look back, look now, and look out into the future. The book of Revelation is said to be blessed for those who study it.

The first book of the Bible is translated as the beginning. We call it Genesis because it is the foundation for understanding Bible prophecy. We can trace our spiritual roots by looking at the beginning and how it all started: the first civilization created, the fall of man, the first murder, the flood, and the tower of Babel.

God announced that he had a plan of salvation, not condemnation. In the middle of God's plan to rescue man, there is Abraham in Genesis, and God focuses on him and his family.

We need to understand the promise of God to Abraham. This is the key to the Bible and to the end time. Two people, Adam and Abraham, are found in the middle of the Bible. We also see two more giants, Ezekiel and Daniel. Ezekiel saw God coming out of the north as a whirlwind of fire, and Daniel had a dream in which he saw four great beasts coming up out of the sea.

The first was a lion with eagle wings on its back. The lion is said to represent Great Britain, and the eagle wings on its back represent the United States. The next beast is a bear with three ribs in its mouth, which represents the country of Russia. The next is a leopard with four heads and wings of a bird on its back. This beast represents Germany, and the bird wings on its back represent France. The last beast has ten horns with iron teeth and iron feet, and it represents Rome.

These are the four countries that will be on Earth when Jesus comes. We go to the end of the Bible, called Revelation, and see two more giants, Paul and John, telling us what the end will be like.

I am glad these giants have left the light on so that I may see my way to the finish line. God has opened the knowledge of these forerunners to blaze the way for us to follow.

In between the Old and the New Testament, we have two roads to take, the express lane or the narrow and rough. God gave man free will to choose which one that you want to take.

For man to have a perfect life, he must obey all of God's rules that are set before him, including all of the commandments of God when he returns to Earth. The Bible gives us three reasons why Christ is returning to Earth. First is He's coming to complete the prophecies of the Bible. Second is Christ is coming to judge the unbelievers, and finally Christ is coming to reclaim Earth that Satan has taken. The signs of the time of the end are present in each generation. The signs of the time will accelerate as we approach the end.

Throughout the Bible, we will be referred to Genesis because in it, we will be pointed in the direction of the cross where it all was paid in full.

It would be music to my ears to hear and know that all of my sins were forgiven on that Friday from the sixth to the ninth hour out on that hill called Calvary.

Thank you, Jesus, for wrapping yourself in human flesh and coming down through the forty-two generations, stopping at Father Abraham.

In order to understand Genesis, we must also consider Psalms 1-41 and how it corresponds to Genesis. The key here is man. Next, we look at Exodus and place Psalms 42-72. The key here is deliverance.

Leviticus is the book of atonement, and Psalms 73-89 deals with the burnt offerings and the worship in the tabernacle. Numbers is the roll call and march, and Psalms 90-106 deals with unrest.

Deuteronomy is the book of remembrance, and Psalms 107-150 deals with God's word and the final preparations for entering the Promised Land.

The historical books are Joshua, Judges, Ruth, 1st and 2nd Samuel, 1st and 2nd Kings, 1st and 2nd Chronicles, Ezra, Nehemiah, and Esther.

The poetry books are Job, Psalms, Proverbs, Ecclesiastes, and Song of Solomon.

The major prophets are Isaiah, Jeremiah, Lamentations, Ezekiel, and Daniel.

Isaiah is a Bible in itself, with 66 chapters, just like the Bible has 66 books. Isaiah 1-39 is called Proto Isaiah and deals with God against man. Isaiah 40-55 is called Deutero Isaiah, and it tells Israel that if they keep their eyes on God, they will never lose hope. Isaiah 56-66 tells Israel that the Gentiles will receive salvation.

Jeremiah is the weeping prophet, and chapter 33-3 is God's direct phone line. Lamentations deals with God's grace. Ezekiel is a faithful preacher who does the exile in Babylon, and he spends 70 years in captivity.

Daniel is the prophet of dreams, and he is known as the bridge between the Old and the New Testaments, preparing the way for Jesus to come.

From Abraham to Christ, there are 42 generations. From Abraham to David, there are 14 generations. From David to the carrying away to Babylon, there are 14 generations. And from the carrying away to Babylon to Christ, there are 14 generations.

Minor Prophets

Hosea, Joel, Amos, Obadiah, Ezra (Edomite), Jonah, Micah, Nahum, Habakkuk, Zephaniah, Haggai, Zechariah, Malachi.

The New Testament has 27 books.

The Gospel stage has four gospel runners: Matthew, Mark, Luke, and John. Matthew's gospel was written to his Jews. Mark's gospel was written to the Romans. Luke's gospel was written to the Greeks. Luke traced his roots back to Adam. John's gospel was different from the others and was written to the world. The gospels of Matthew, Mark, and Luke are known as the Synoptic Gospels because they can be viewed together.

Acts tells the story of the early church and the birth of the church.

The Epistles stage is by Paul and includes Romans, 1st and 2nd Corinthians, Galatians, Ephesians, Philippians, Colossians, 1st and 2nd Thessalonians, 1st and 2nd Timothy, Titus, and Philemon.

The General Epistles are Hebrews, James, 1st and 2nd Peter, 1st, 2nd, and 3rd John, and the letter of Jude.

The prophecy of Revelation tells us what was seen, what is happening now, and what will happen in the future.

www.ingramcontent.com/pod-product-compliance
Lightning Source LLC
Chambersburg PA
CBHW031302120626
46545CB00007B/2943